i—
portraits
of
anarchists

ACKNOWLEDGEMENTS

Thanks for all the help given by Dean at AK Press, Alice Nutter, Boff and Paula Emery. Thanks also to all the anarchists, including those not included in this collection.

casey orr

I - PORTRAITS OF ANARCHISTS

First printing 1996 in an edition of 2500
Copyright © 1996 casey orr
Printed by Calverts, London, UK

Chumbawamba music copyright © 1996 One Little Indian Ltd, 250 York Road, London SW11 3SJ

ISBN 1-873176-376

Typesetting & design by Baader-Meinhof 1996

Partially funded by Yorkshire & Humberside Arts

British Library cataloguing-in-publication data
A CIP catalogue record for this book is available from the British Library

Library of Congress cataloguing-in-publication data
A catalogue record for this title is available from the Library of Congress

Distributed in bookshops in UK and Europe by
AK Distribution
PO Box 12766
Edinburgh
EH8 9YE
Scotland

in USA by
AK Press
PO Box 40682
San Francisco
CA 94140 - 0682
USA

Send large SAE to AK Press for full catalogue of titles

PUBLISHED (AND DISTRIBUTED AS A CD) BY
ONE LITTLE INDIAN
250 YORK ROAD
LONDON
SW11 3SJ

i-ntroduction

There's a fundamental problem with photographing anarchists; a problem rooted in the gap between what we see and what we know. For perhaps it's only what we think we know. The starting point for these portraits, taken throughout 1994 and 1995, is to present something real, tangible and visible which clashes furiously with preconception. Anarchists: media shorthand for those who engineer anti-social chaos. We know what to expect. These photographs, in their straightforward, gentle strength, show instead something of all of us, a tightrope walked between the everyday and the unusual.

The photographs in "i" catch a cross-section and hold it still for a while. There areoccasional glimpses of the passions and anger which fuel the delicate faces, and there are also sly betrayals of their absolute *normalness* . It's between these poles that this collection of portraits rests. Harsh words, gentle smiles; brooding eyes, eloquent speech.

Somewhere in the space between the camera and the subject are a million myths. Hopefully these photographs dismantle some of those myths, if only by Casey Orr's insistence on capturing people as people, not specimens. Preconceptions make us feel safe - they *don't* make good photographs. Preconceptions are badly-focussed, ill-framed. Casey Orr's anarchists thus defy what the world expects; here we see vulnerability and energy within the same photograph, a collection of portraits which belong together through anarchism's aknowledging (and celebration of) differences.

Real history is made by those whose lives go unrecorded. Photographs, in turn, can sometimes pass down a moment, can record something outside both our memories and expectations.. to this end, "i" is a glimpse of some of the people and ideas which make up late twentieth century anarchism. "i" isn't a record of self-obsession; it's about the bond between individuality - the anarchist's love of absolute freedom - and a desire to work together. Me, you. Photographer and subject. Photograph and viewer.

Photography is sometimes guilty of showing a world where people are divided into movements, gangs, tribes and eccentrics, people who can be studied under a microscope but never move in next door. If Casey's collection of anarchist portraits say anything at all, it's that any of these people may be living next door *right now.*

Which brings us part way to solving that initial problem - what we see, what we know. Anarchism, here not a manifesto or a news headline but a calmly beautiful collection of black & white photographs, is far removed from that one-dimensional idea the media fixes it with. As the portraits suggest, it is both vulnerable and strong, simple and complex, ordinary and weird. "i" comes not to reinforce a sensational myth, but to present a tangible reality. Which is one of the best things a collection of photographs can do...

chumbawamba

about the music
chumbawamba

THE CD ACCOMPANYING THIS BOOK WAS RECORDED AT VARIOUS TIMES DURING 1995. THE SONGS WERE WRITTEN IN RESPONSE TO BOTH THE PHOTOGRAPHS AND TO THE INTERVIEWS WITH THE PEOPLE BEING PHOTOGRAPHED. THE WORDS DRAW ON SPECIFICALLY ANARCHIST IDEAS; THE MUSIC PUT TOGETHER WITHOUT RELYING ON CHUMBAWAMBA'S "USUAL" INSTRUMENTATION. THANKS TO NEIL FERGUSON, THE ENGINEER AT WOODLANDS STUDIO, AND TO RAPHAEL FROM POLAND FOR THE SNIPPET OF CONVERSATION PRECEDING *SO MUCH*.

don't tip-toe **1**

nothing knocks me over **2**

i can only give / take so much **3**

i am tradition & tomorrow **4**

time after time **5**

you grow old **6**

TOTAL TIME: 17'15"
WRITTEN & PRODUCED BY CHUMBAWAMBA
PUBLISHED BY CHUMBAWAMBA(LEOSONG)

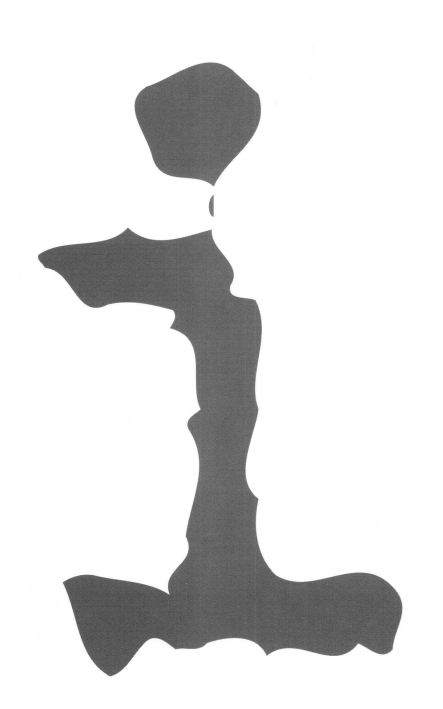

CLAUDIA

writer, london, uk

"I'VE GOT GREAT AUNTIES IN THEIR EIGHTIES WHO DON'T GIVE A FUCK WHAT ANYBODY THINKS. THAT'S MY AMBITION... NOT TO GIVE A FUCK."

(PAINTER, NEW YORK, USA)

"i remember a talk i gave in the 1930's to 500 steelworkers in youngstown, ohio. the biggest hit was the iww songbook... if we'd had more strength we could have made a significant impact – because workers are sympathetic to anarchism."

MARIANNA

(FASHION DESIGNER, MEXICO CITY, MEXICO)

"my grandfather was an anarchist. my mother conceived me and then went to jail for her beliefs. anarchism is in my blood."

(Counceller/Advice
worker, Adult Educator
London, uk)

" David: I saw him across the room at a party and thought 'who is that distinguished gentleman?'. It was lust at first sight rather than political ideas! I've fancied people who are gorgeous but they've opened their mouths and been ignorant bigots - I've wanted to smack them in the mouth more than sleep with them."

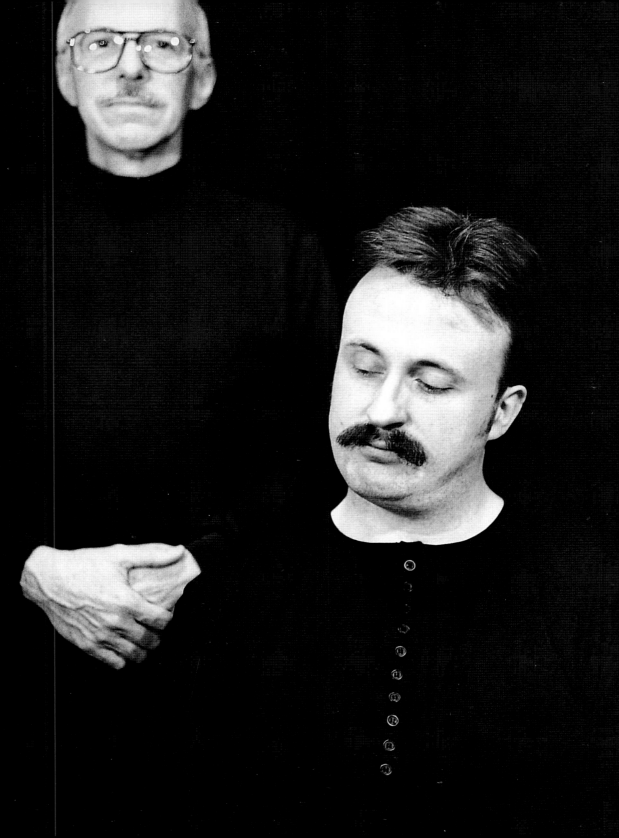

pete the roady (BAND ROADY, BATH, UK)

" I LIKE PUTTING PEOPLE UP AND MUCKING IN. "

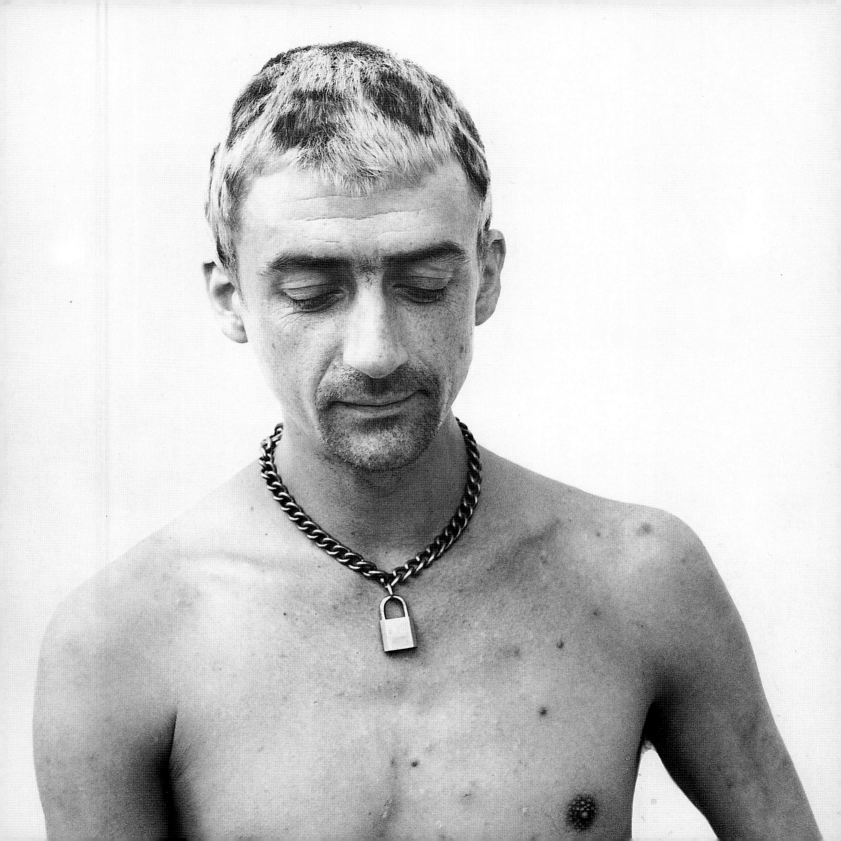

janet biehl

(Free-lance Editor, Burlington, Vermont, USA)

"ANARCHISM TO ME HAS ALWAYS BEEN AN IDEAL OF SOCIAL FREEDOM, ONE TO WHICH I HAVE STEADFASTLY ADHERED THROUGHOUT MY LIFE."

chuck morse

(Political philosophy student, New York, USA)

"when I was 14 I accompanied my father on a business trip to London. and from then on I've been an anarchist. I was so convinced of the possibility of anarchism that I felt that I only had to mention to other people the possibility of an anarchist way of life... so as soon as my father woke up the following day I immediately did that and he immediately disregarded it and told me he didn't think it was realistic. and that was my first political lesson: that the task of political education has to encounter great resistance."

DOLF

(independent promoter, auschburg, germany)

"I like being independent. I can't imagine working for the music industry. I might as well become a pimp."

carmell c

(ecology student, puerto rican now residing in vermont. usa

"liberalism is smart.they take the leaders of the protest movements and give them government jobs. that's it. it's over. they start to moderate their rhetoric as soon as their individual interest is served."

Celine

(ACTIVIST, PARIS, FRANCE)

"when I was 17 i read emma goldman. I thought, I can do that..."

frank, bettan, mia, tania

(Accountant, Community Worker, Schoolchildren, Leeds, UK)

"

I hope my kids learn not to respect authority just because it's there."

tuppy owens
(sexpert, london, uk)

" AS A CHILD I SHARED MY SWEETIES. AS PEOPLE GROW UP THEY STOP; I'M STILL SHARING MINE."

Jay Brophy

(l a b o u r e r ,   l o s   a n g e l e s ,   u s a)

As a worker I think it's outrageous that I'm still working 8 hours a day. The whole

"

Libertarian idea of why we are working so much I think is the key to why anarchism should

be involved in the labour movement. Most people have jobs because they have to put food

on the table and a roof over their heads; and in return they're supposed to spend what they

make on the shit that they produce. There are other things to be done with our time."

PAULA EMERY

(education and garment worker, vermont, usa)

" For me it's about experiencing joy and pleasure. Capitalism is destroying us and it's destroying the whole planet. I like to flaunt that I'm not going to let it destroy me."

merwyn 16(musician, london, uk)

"When the cops got a kicking at Trafalgar Square, I was, like, 'Yes!' I love it when the bad guys don't win."

" i think i'm very brave... sometimes too brave for my own good."

3 04165 66 32061

kellen
(Coordinator of an S&M legal defence group, London, UK)

"

WHEN WE ALLOW PEOPLE TO HAVE RESPONSIBILITY, LIKE TREASURERS AND SECRETARIES, WE SHOULD HAVE CONTROL OVER THEM. NO-ONE SHOULD HAVE PRIVILEGE JUST FOR BEING AN ORGANISER."

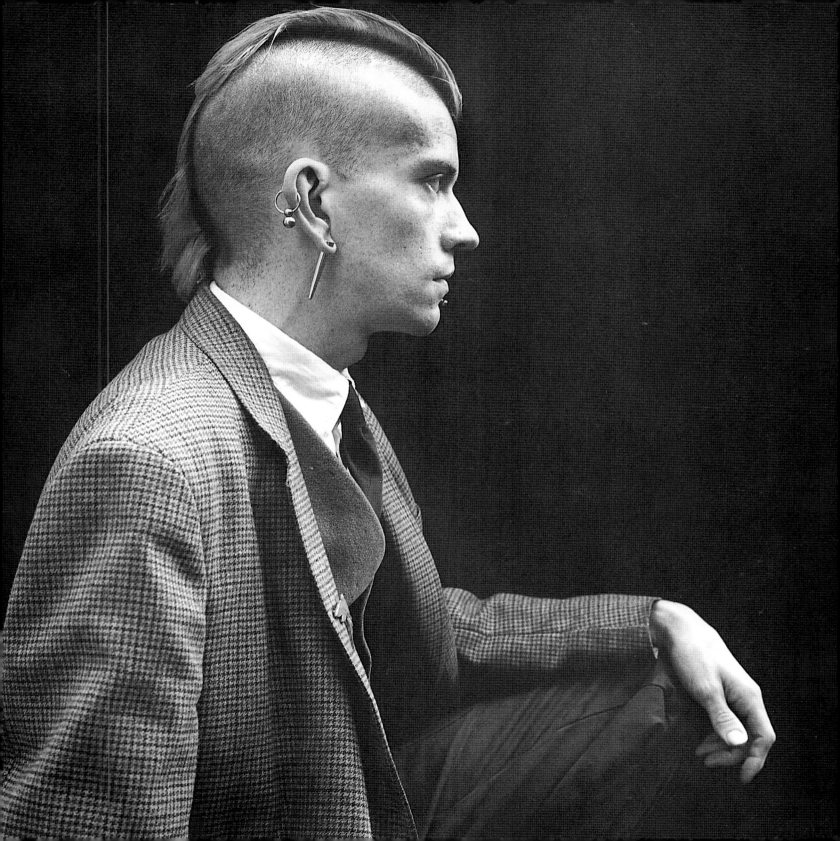

MURRAY BOOKCHIN (Writer, lecturer, Vermont, USA)

" *Peter Kropotkin described Anarchism as the extreme left wing of socialism*

- a view with which I completely agree. One of my deepest concerns today

is that the libertarian socialist core will be eroded by fashionable, post-

modernist, spiritualist, mystic individualism."

steve kinky

(RADICAL FASHION DESIGNER, LONDON, UK)

"*We're not going to give you nice little labels and a pigeonhole for us. There's not going to be a convenient tag so that the voyeuristic vampires of friendly weird capitalism can build their careers by having our culture stuffed and put on display in museums such as the V & A or the ICA.*"

Marrissa Carr (Sex performer, London, UK)

"Coming from a nice Jewish family, I've always been obsessed with sleaze; dirty things. There's a collective imagination among our generation of women with what's supposed to be bad."

Zoe

(Vancouver BC, Canada)

I CAME TO ANARCHISM THROUGH BEING HOMELESS.
POLITICS ISN'T JUST
THEORY WHEN YOU'VE
NOWHERE TO LIVE.

ROZ BEAUHILL

(Explorer, Bristol, uk)

"*I ended up having all these kids, working and being an unsupported mother... and the idea of personal empowerment always stayed with me.*"

a l b e r t   m e l t z e r

(RETIRED PRINTWORKER,
LONDON, ENGLAND)

" When I worked in print we earned more than management, but we were still working class. It's what you know, who you identify with. People mistake affluence for class."

(book editor and publisher, new york, usa) matt black

" WHAT ARE THE SOCIAL PROCESSES BY WHICH PEOPLES' SENSE OF THEIR ABILITY TO ACT IS MAXIMISED? I PERSONALLY THINK IT'S PARTICIPATION IN SOCIAL MOVEMENTS. THAT PEOPLE FIND THEMSELVES IN OPPOSITION TO SOCIETY FOR WHATEVER REASON, AND GO FROM OPPOSITION TO REVOLT AGAINST SOCIETY. OPPOSITION HAPPENS QUITE NATURALLY DUE TO EXISTING SOCIAL TENSIONS. BUT THE MOVE TO REVOLT COMBINES SOCIAL PRESSURES AND A DESIRE TO ACT. THE ROLE OF REVOLUTIONARIES IS TO ARGUE FOR ACTION AND FOR A SPECIFIC POLITICS. IT DOESN'T COME FROM OUTSIDE, BUT BECAUSE WE'RE ACTUALLY PART OF THE PROCESS. "

D•I•Y

(dj collective, nottingham, uk)

dance music has always had an unreality, of being unconnected to social problems; we tried to evolve into a collective that was still politically responsible. it's the unspoken ideology of liberation through fun."

CLARA SOLOMON (Pianist, New York, USA)

When I was a girl, it was at home that I heard discussions about unions and strikes and Anarchist activities. Peter Kropotkin, Errico Malatesta, Emma Goldman, and Rudolf Rocker were household names. In the middle 1920's Rudolf and Millie Rocker stayed with us in our home when they came to lecture in Stelton, New Jersey. This made an enduring impression on my brothers Sigmund and David... and me, of course."

Daniel Chodorkoff

(co-founder and director of the institute for social ecology, marshfield, vermont, usa)

"I BELIEVE IN ANARCHISM BECAUSE IT IS THE PHILOSOPHY WHICH HOLDS THE BEST HOPE FOR FINDING A BALANCE BETWEEN THE FREE DEVELOPMENT OF THE INDIVIDUAL AND THE EMPOWERMENT OF THE COMMUNITY. IT REPRESENTS AN IDEAL TOWARD WHICH WE MUST CONSTANTLY STRIVE."

avi pitchon
(artist, tel aviv, israel)

"UNITY ISN'T UNIFORMITY OR CONFORMITY; BUT I KNOW WHY I SOMETIMES LIKE TO DRESS IN A UNIFORM WAY. I LIKE THE SENSE OF BELONGING TO A TRIBE."

RODRIGO

(plumber, orleans, france)

" **anarchy for me, it's a way of living. I don't ask myself what it is - it's a part of me.** "

georgia & helen

(DJS, LEEDS, UK)

"REVENGE IS A BIG THING. ALL THE PEOPLE WHO SPOUT SEXIST CLICHES AT US AND GET IN OUR WAY: WE WILL GET EVEN WITH THEM EVENTUALLY."

jon langford

(musician,
chicago,
usa)

"I was such an optimistic kid. I'm an anarchist because
I'm angry about not being able to be an astronaut."

CHICKEN

(fanzine editor, allentown, pennsylvania, usa)

Every time I go to something I hear 'Oh, what are you doing with your life now? Are you in college? Do you have a job?' No! I'm just trying to deal with life and I can't just jump into things - I'm not gonna kow-tow to any job that gives a quarter of my salary to someone I've never met."

suzy

(Graphic Designer, Rome, Italy)

"

in italy, not looking italian is enough for people to be hostile. not to dress like everyone else too means that you are really hated.

raymond

(RETIRED TEXTILE WORKER, LONDON, UK)

" I WORE THIS CAPE WHEN I TOOK JOHNNY TO VISIT HIS FATHER IN A BUDAPEST PRISON. THE NAZIS WERE GOING TO SHIP HIM TO A CONCENTRATION CAMP. JOHNNY ASKED THE HUNGARIAN POLICEMAN 'WHEN ARE YOU GOING TO LET MY FATHER COME HOME?' HE NEVER DID."

jake prescott

(rights worker, bradford, uk)

"

I spent fifteen years in prison for being
involved with the Angry Brigade... La Lotta
Continua!"

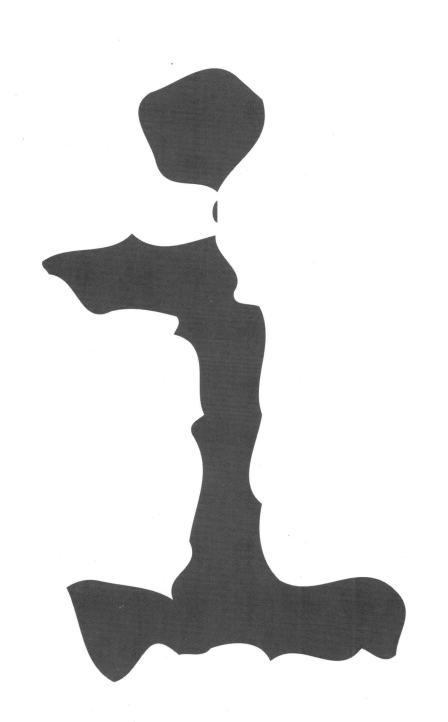